WA

WHARFEDALE

HILLSIDE GUIDES

LONG DISTANCE WALKS

1 • THE WESTMORLAND WAY
2 • THE FURNESS WAY
3 • THE CUMBERLAND WAY
7 • CLEVELAND WAY COMPANION
9 • THE NORTH BOWLAND TRAVERSE
    (by David Johnson)
16 • DALES WAY COMPANION

CIRCULAR WALKS - YORKSHIRE DALES

4 • WALKS IN WHARFEDALE
5 • WALKS IN NIDDERDALE
6 • WALKS IN THE CRAVEN DALES
8 • WALKS IN WENSLEYDALE
10 • WALKS IN THREE PEAKS COUNTRY
11 • WALKS IN SWALEDALE
20 • RAMBLES IN WHARFEDALE
21 • WALKS ON THE HOWGILL FELLS

CIRCULAR WALKS - NORTH YORK MOORS

13 • WESTERN - Cleveland/Hambleton Hills
14 • SOUTHERN - Rosedale/Farndale/Bransdale
15 • NORTHERN - Eskdale and the Coast

CIRCULAR WALKS - SOUTH PENNINES

12 • WALKS IN BRONTE COUNTRY
17 • WALKS IN CALDERDALE

HILLWALKING - THE LAKE DISTRICT

18 • OVER LAKELAND MOUNTAINS
19 • OVER LAKELAND FELLS

———

FREEDOM OF THE DALES
40 selected walks
Full colour hardback

WALKS
IN
WHARFEDALE

by

Paul Hannon

HILLSIDE  PUBLICATIONS

HILLSIDE PUBLICATIONS
11 Nessfield Grove
Exley Head
Keighley
West Yorkshire
BD22 6NU

First published 1985
Revised 1988
6th impression 1991

Page 1 illustration: At Linton

ISBN 1 870141 07 5

Printed in Great Britain by
Carnmor Print and Design
95/97 London Road
Preston
Lancashire
PR1 4BA

INTRODUCTION

The subject of this book is the upper valley of the river Wharfe, from the boundary of the Yorkshire Dales National Park at Bolton Bridge to beyond Buckden: included is the quieter side-valley of Littondale. Wharfedale is the most popular valley in the Dales, this being attributable not least of all to its accessibility. The West Yorkshire cities of Leeds and Bradford and their surrounding towns are but a modest distance away, and on summer weekends the banks of the river see as many sun-worshippers as ramblers.

The Wharfe's name originates from the Celtic meaning 'swift water', and this lovely river races for almost 30 miles from Beckermonds to Bolton Bridge before a rather more sedate run to join the Ouse near Selby. At Beckermonds the Wharfe is made by the confluence of Oughtershaw and Green Field Becks, which have themselves already covered some distance from the lonely heights of Cam Fell.

The Wharfe's major tributary is the Skirfare, which flows through — and sometimes beneath — its own dale, Littondale to lose its identity near the famous landmark of Kilnsey Crag. Though Littondale has many characteristics of its big brother, it is separated by steep-sided fells and its seclusion gives it an intimate, possibly even greater charm.

North of Kilnsey the valley floors are dead flat and never more than half a mile wide, and at a very clearly-defined boundary the fells begin their majestic rise to numerous 2000-foot summits. At regular intervals their slopes are scored by crystal clear mountain becks which have a short-lived but very joyful journey. While the higher tops display the gritstone features of peat groughs and never-dry terrain, the lower slopes show off the ever-fascinating scars of gleaming limestone.

Lower down the dale meanwhile, gritstone dominates in the huge forms of Barden Moor and Fell. These extensive areas of rolling heather moorland face each other across the Wharfe, and together are valued grouse shooting country. Happily they are the subject of a negotiated access agreement with the land-owner (the Duke of Devonshire's estates) and walkers are free to roam over the upland areas subject to various restrictions.

The main point is that the moors can be 'closed' on certain days when shooting takes place, though not Sundays. Although notices are posted at the access points (along with a list of all restrictions) disappointment can be avoided by ringing the estate office beforehand (Bolton Abbey 227). Also worth knowing—dogs are not allowed. *Walks 1 and 15 take advantage of this facility.*

5

THE ROAD NETWORK

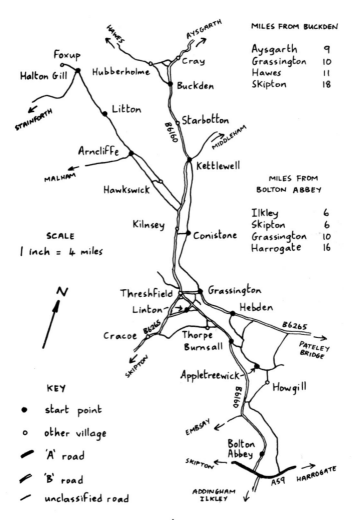

MILES FROM BUCKDEN

Aysgarth	9
Grassington	10
Hawes	11
Skipton	18

MILES FROM BOLTON ABBEY

Ilkley	6
Skipton	6
Grassington	10
Harrogate	16

SCALE
1 inch = 4 miles

N

KEY

- ● start point
- ○ other village
- ━ 'A' road
- ╱ 'B' road
- ╱ unclassified road

Foxup
Halton Gill
Hubberholme
Cray
Buckden
Litton
Starbotton
Arncliffe
Kettlewell
Hawkswick
Kilnsey
Conistone
Threshfield
Grassington
Linton
Hebden
Cracoe
Thorpe
Burnsall
Appletreewick
Howgill
Bolton Abbey

HAWES
AYSGARTH
STAINFORTH
MALHAM
MIDDLEHAM
B6160
B6265
PATELEY BRIDGE
SKIPTON
EMBSAY
B6160
B6265
SKIPTON
ADDINGHAM ILKLEY
A59
HARROGATE

6

The 16 walks described range in length from 3½ to 9 miles, and the terrain similarly varies from riverside strolls to rather more strenous moorland walking. All walks are circular, and with an average distance of 6¼ miles are ideally suited to half-day rambles. Each walk is given its own chapter consisting of 'immediate impression' diagram, detailed narrative and strip-map and notes and illustrations of features of interest along the way.

Overleaf are listed the various facilities which can be found in the valley. There is ample accommodation in a variety of forms, including many of the inns. The vast majority of the villages have at least one licensed house, and virtually all are comfortable, well-kept establishments which lean heavily towards the visitor. The provision of food is as regular – and important – a feature as the availability of traditional beers.

Wharfedale has two conveniently sited youth hostels, with Linton serving the lower dale and Kettlewell covering the upper valley. Both also cater for walkers on the Dales Way, a long-distance route which runs the length of the dale, clinging largely to the riverbank before crossing into Dentdale. Bunk-barn accommodation is on the increase, and there are several camping sites in the valley.

The nearest railway station down the valley is at the cul-de-sac of Ilkley, though the station at Skipton is usually more accessible. It is also from Skipton that the dale is best served by bus, with the main service being to Grassington. In summer months some visitor-orientated services may well be found.

Grassington is the largest centre with a good range of shops, but it is the thriving market town of Skipton that really serves the dale: the market can be found on the following days – Monday, Wednesday, Friday and Saturday. Early-closing days are Grassington, Thursday ; Skipton, Tuesday; Ilkley, Wednesday.

ORDNANCE SURVEY MAPS

Although the strip-maps illustrating each walk are sufficient to guide one safely around, they show nothing of the surrounding countryside. An Ordnance Survey map will provide the answer.

1:50,000 Landranger : sheets 98 and 104

Greater detail is shown on the Outdoor Leisure maps, sheets 10 and 30 covering the entire area.

7

SOME USEFUL FACILITIES

	Accommodation	Inn	Car park	Bus service	Post office	other shop	WC	Payphone
Appletreewick	✓	✓		✓	✓			✓
Arncliffe	✓	✓		✓	✓			✓
Bolton Abbey	✓	✓	✓	✓	✓	✓	✓	✓
Buckden	✓	✓	✓	✓	✓	✓	✓	✓
Burnsall	✓	✓	✓	✓	✓	✓	✓	✓
Conistone				✓				✓
Cracoe	✓	✓		✓		✓		✓
Cray	✓	✓						
Grassington	✓	✓	✓	✓	✓	✓	✓	✓
Halton Gill								✓
Hawkswick	✓							
Hebden	✓	✓		✓	✓		✓	✓
Howgill	✓			✓		✓		✓
Hubberholme	✓	✓						
Kettlewell	✓	✓	✓	✓	✓	✓	✓	✓
Linton	✓	✓	✓	✓	✓		✓	✓
Litton	✓	✓			✓			✓
Starbotton	✓	✓		✓				✓
Thorpe	✓							
Threshfield	✓	✓		✓				✓

SOME USEFUL ADDRESSES

Ramblers' Association
   1/5 Wandsworth Road, London SW8 2XX
      Tel. 071 - 582 6878

Youth Hostels Association
   Trevelyan House, St. Albans, Herts. AL1 2DY
      Tel. 0727 - 55215

Yorkshire Dales National Park Office
   Colvend, Hebden Road, Grassington,
   Skipton, North Yorkshire BD23 5LB
      Tel. 0756 - 752748

Grassington National Park Centre
   Hebden Road, Grassington
      Tel. 0756 - 752774

Ilkley Tourist Information
   Station Road, Ilkley
      Tel. 0943 - 602319

Skipton Tourist Information
   Victoria Square, Skipton
      Tel. 0756 - 792809

Yorkshire Dales Society
   Otley Civic Centre, Cross Green, Otley LS21 1HD
      Tel. 0943 - 607868

Keighley and District Travel
   Central Buildings, Keighley Road, Skipton
      Tel. 0756 - 795331

Yorkshire Dales weather — 0898 - 500 748

THE WALKS

Listed below are the 16 walks described, the walk number being the Key to easy location in the guide

THE WALKS

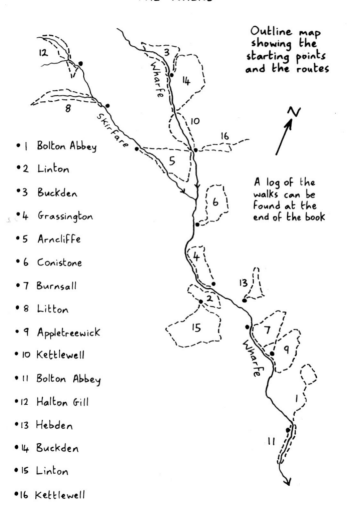

Outline map
showing the
starting points
and the routes

N

A log of the
walks can be
found at the
end of the book

- 1 Bolton Abbey
- 2 Linton
- 3 Buckden
- 4 Grassington
- 5 Arncliffe
- 6 Conistone
- 7 Burnsall
- 8 Litton
- 9 Appletreewick
- 10 Kettlewell
- 11 Bolton Abbey
- 12 Halton Gill
- 13 Hebden
- 14 Buckden
- 15 Linton
- 16 Kettlewell

WALK 1

8½ miles

THE ASCENT OF SIMON'S SEAT

from Bolton Abbey

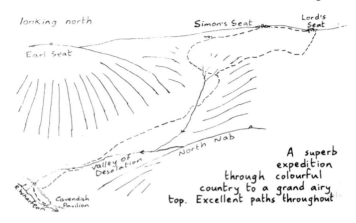

looking north

A superb expedition through colourful country to a grand airy top. Excellent paths throughout

This is the only walk in the book to return by what is largely the same route.

The most suitable starting point is the Cavendish Pavilion. It is signposted off the B6160 just north of Bolton Abbey, turning off by the large memorial fountain.

THE WALK

Leave the Pavilion by crossing the wooden bridge over the river and immediately taking a path upstream. Entering some trees it soon emerges onto a narrow road at Posforth Bridge. Double back up the hill to a clearing at the top, and forsake the road for a gate on the left by an access notice. Head half-left across the pasture past some hoary oaks to a gate, from where a good track crosses to reach Posforth Gill. While the main path turns right to run along the rim of the drop to the beck, a detour down to it will be well repaid with a close-up view of the waterfall.

Having witnessed the spectacle the beck might be forded and the north bank followed upstream, though the usual path remains on the same side to cross by a tiny footbridge a little further up. Soon a fork is reached: although our way rises to the left, another brief diversion is recommended, simply continuing upstream to enjoy an equally lovely waterfall. The main path, meanwhile, rises to a stile to enter Laund Pasture Plantation. A wide track leads rapidly to the far end of the trees, where a gate admits onto the open moor.

A good, clear track heads directly away, and leads unerringly to the summit of Simon's Seat. On the way there it fords Great Agill Beck prior to a short, steep section. Beyond a stone table a shooter's track branches off to the right: this is where we rejoin the outward route on returning from the top. Our ascending path crosses the headwaters of the beck before swinging right to pass Truckle Crags, and the large grouping of rocks atop Simon's Seat are only a couple of minutes away.

The environs of the summit are a source of potential confusion in bad visibility, but the presence of a footpath sign at the nearby path junction helps avoid this possibility. The unmistakeable form of an Ordnance Survey column adorns the highest rocks, and to add interest to the final few feet, hands must be used to attain it.

To vary the return take the sketchy path heading east to the prominent outcrops of Lord's Seat, then turn right alongside the wall immediately behind. After a short half-mile of gradual descent turn sharp right along a shooter's track. This wide track undulates across the moor and leads unfailingly back to the outward route near the stone table. Steps can now be happily retraced all the way back to the Pavilion.

The title 'Valley of Desolation' could not be less appropriate to the colourful terrain here.

The view from Simon's Seat is made unforgettable by virtue of our sheltered line of approach, keeping all to the north hidden until the very last moment. Along with the anticipated distant panorama is a dramatic birds-eye view of the valley below, a result of the unbroken plunge of the northern slope of the fell. The environs of Skyreholme and Appletreewick form a splendid picture, with Trollers Gill, Parceval Hall and Grimwith Reservoir easily located. A nice section of the Wharfe itself can also be seen. See also the diagram overleaf.

The giant boulders of Simon's Seat and Lord's Seat make an ideal playground for scramblers.

* From this stone table Truckle Crags and more distantly Simon's Seat come into view.

SIMON'S SEAT 1591'

OS column 55294

Truckle Crags

Lord's Seat 1565'

④

Hen Stones

Great Agill Head

③

⑤

Great Agill Beck

* butts

⑥

ford

N

Apart from the vicinity of Simon's Seat, this walk remains a good, dry one, even after above average rain.

The waterfall, Posforth Gill

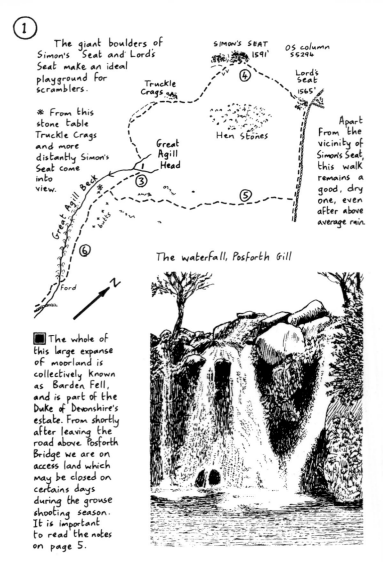

■ The whole of this large expanse of moorland is collectively known as Barden Fell, and is part of the Duke of Devonshire's estate. From shortly after leaving the road above Posforth Bridge we are on access land which may be closed on certains days during the grouse shooting season. It is important to read the notes on page 5.

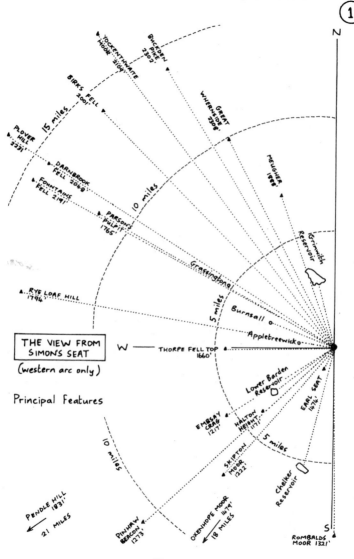

THE VIEW FROM SIMONS SEAT
(western arc only)

Principal Features

N

YOCKENTHWAITE MOOR 2109'
BUCKDEN PIKE 2302'
BIRKS FELL 2001'
GREAT WHERNSIDE 2306'
PLOVER HILL 2231'
MEUGHER 1689'
15 miles
DARNBROOK FELL 2068'
FOUNTAINS FELL 2191'
10 miles
PARSONS PULPIT 1765'
Grimwith Reservoir
Grassington
RYE LOAF HILL 1796'
5 miles
Burnsall
Appletreewick
W — THORPE FELL TOP 1660'
Lower Barden Reservoir
EARL SEAT 1414'
EMBSAY CRAG 1217'
HALTON HEIGHT 1171'
SKIPTON MOOR 1222'
Chelker Reservoir
10 miles
5 miles
PENDLE HILL 1831' 21 MILES
PINHAW BEACON 1273'
OXENHOPE MOOR 1474' 18 MILES
ROMBALDS MOOR 1321'
S

WALK 2

3½ miles

from Linton Falls

A mere stroll through the fields,
with a host of interesting features.

There is a small car-park on the
cul-de-sac road to Linton Church.

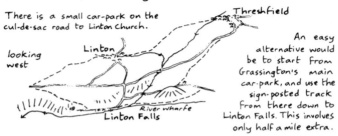

An easy
alternative would
be to start from
Grassington's main
car-park, and use the
sign-posted track
from there down to
Linton Falls. This involves
only half a mile extra.

THE WALK

From the car park head back along the road for
a short distance, and after the last house turn down to the
right in a ginnel leading to the Tin Bridge across the Wharfe.
After surveying the turbulent falls immediately downstream, turn
back a few yards to cross the little pack-bridge over a similarly
tiny stream. Now pass to the right of the cottage to accompany
the Wharfe upstream, soon being channelled up to a stile onto
a road. Now turn left the short distance to Threshfield school.
Take a gate immediately after the schoolyard and head up the
field on a track which swings right to a bridge across the
former railway line. It then continues away from it to run a
little sketchily to a gate onto another road. Turn right then
first left to enter the centre of old Threshfield.

At the end of the road turn left to join the main
road as it descends to Threshfield Bridge. Immediately after
the buildings on the other side escape by a stile on the left to
rise diagonally up the field to a gateway. Follow the wall away
from it to pass through a tree-fringed wall, then continue
straight across the next field to a footbridge back over the
former railway line. Bear half-right down the field to a wall
corner shrouded in trees, where a gate gives access to an
enclosed track. Running parallel with Linton Beck to the left,
it leads unfailingly to the road through Linton village.

Turn briefly right and then sharp left between

the green and the whitewashed inn. A choice of beck-crossings conveys us to the opposite lane, which is followed to the right to within yards of its demise. Here turn left in front of a barn and along a short enclosed track. Soon it breaks free, and is rapidly vacated by means of a stile on the left. Stay with the left-hand wall until it begins to drop away, then contour round to the right: down to the left now is the former Linton residential school. On reaching a cross-wall, the first of four stiles on virtually the same contour is encountered. After the last of these - a fine old work of art hidden in a corner - drop down to the left to a gate onto the Threshfield-Burnsall road again.

Turn right along the road for a few yards only to a gate on the opposite side, then head diagonally across two narrow fields with gap-stiles. Continue the direction to near the top corner of a plantation, but remain above the steep drop towards Linton church and the river, instead going across to the far corner of the field. A stile will be found to the right of a barn: from it continue on through a meadow to its far corner, there joining a short, enclosed way emerging back onto the road. Before returning to the car park, turn right to visit the church, now only two minutes away.

The Church
of St. Michael
and All Angels,
Linton

Linton is generally accepted as being one of northern England's most attractive villages, and not without good reason. A rich assortment of limestone buildings stand in very laid-back fashion, none wishing to crowd the spacious green. Nearest is the whitewashed little hostelry, whose name recalls a local benefactor: Richard Fountaine made his money in London, but in his will he remembered Linton by paying for the 'hospital' at the end of the green. This 18th century building is still in use as almshouses. Through the green runs Linton Beck, crossed in quick succession by a road bridge, a ford, a clapper bridge and most strikingly, a packhorse bridge.

Threshfield is a disjointed village scattered in various directions around the junction of the Skipton-Grassington road with the main up-dale road. The 'new' part of the village - with its striking Catholic church of modern design - is along the road towards Grassington, but it is the more interesting old corner we visit. Solid stone cottages and farm buildings overlook a quaint, triangular green, enclosed by walls and shrouded in trees. Inside are some stocks and the flowers of spring.

On turning alongside the green note the stone lintel of the old post office, dated 1651. Just across the main road is the popular inn, whose title serves to indicate its original purpose.

Passed earlier in the walk is the village school, which was built in the 17th century as a grammar school.

The former railway was a branch line from Skipton to Grassington, and was in use from 1902 to 1969. It still comes within a couple of miles, but only to serve a quarry.

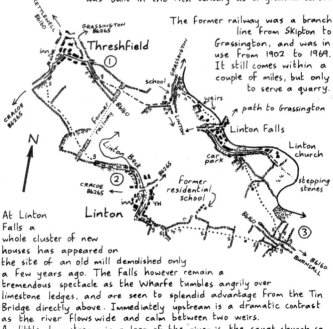

At Linton Falls a whole cluster of new houses has appeared on the site of an old mill demolished only a few years ago. The Falls however remain a tremendous spectacle as the Wharfe tumbles angrily over limestone ledges, and are seen to splendid advantage from the Tin Bridge directly above. Immediately upstream is a dramatic contrast as the river flows wide and calm between two weirs.

A little downstream in a loop of the river is the squat church, so positioned as to be central to the several villages it was built to serve. Dating from Norman times, it retains much 15th century work and its lovely interior lives up to its idyllic setting.

WALK 3

HUBBERHOLME, CRAY AND SCAR TOP

5 miles

from Buckden

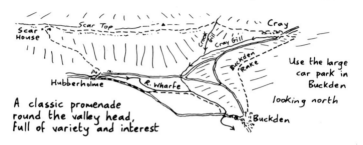

Use the large car park in Buckden

looking north

A classic promenade round the valley head, full of variety and interest

THE WALK

Leave the car park not by its usual exit, instead use a gate at its northern end from where a stony track gently rises up Buckden Rake. At the end of the surround of trees it turns right through a gate to commence a pleasant, level section. On drawing level with the buildings of Cray down to the left, take a gate in the adjacent wall and drop down a steep field to another gate from where Cray Gill is forded to join the road right next to the inn.

To leave Cray take the farm track immediately behind the hostelry and follow it up to the left, keeping to the right of the various farm buildings. Having passed through a gate above the last building the way remains level through several fields, becoming indistinct but aiming for a barn just ahead. Go to the left of it to then swing right to a tiny footbridge over Crook Gill.

From the footbridge swing left to commence a long, easy mile above the well-defined escarpment cloaked in trees on the left: part-way along, the stately Wharfedale Cairn beckons just up to the right. All too soon the path arrives just above Scar House. Turn down between the buildings to accompany the stony access road down the hillside into Hubberholme, emerging alongside the church.

For the final leg of the walk cross the bridge over the Wharfe to the inn, and if not delayed there turn to the left along the road. After about half a mile take a gate on the left to rejoin the river, which is now accompanied downdale to soon reach Buckden Bridge. Join the road to recross the river and so arrive back in Buckden village.

Buckden is the first sizeable settlement encountered by the Wharfe, and stands at the meeting place of two high roads from Wensleydale to the north. The good quality B6160 comes via Cray to take over as the valley road from the narrow, winding road that reaches nearly 2000 feet on its way over Fleet Moss from Hawes, before running through Langstrothdale to get to Buckden. In medieval times Buckden was the centre of a vast hunting forest, and its hostelry recalls its former importance in its name. The village stands high above the river on the slope of Buckden Pike, and swift-flowing Buckden Beck carves a deep defile down from the summit.

Buckden Pike from the Wharfedale Cairn

Though barely even a hamlet, Hubberholme boasts two famous buildings and a shapely bridge which connects them. The church of St. Michael is a gem, its tower showing Norman traces. Its best feature is a 500 year old oak rood loft, one of only two remaining in Yorkshire, while some pews bear the famous trademark of 'Mousey' Thompson. Carving therefore – both ancient and modern – dominates the interior of this highest church in the dale. Outside, meanwhile, the sparkling Wharfe runs almost past its very door.

Across the river is the whitewashed and homely George Inn in an idyllic setting. Formerly housing the vicar, its flagged floors continued to be the scene of the New Year 'land-letting' when proceeds of a 'poor pasture' go to needy parishioners.

Restored last century, the isolated Scar House was the scene of early Quaker gatherings.

Situated at over 1000 feet above sea level, the farming hamlet of Cray is the last outpost of Wharfedale on the high road over to Bishopdale and ultimately Wensleydale. This crossing of the fells is known as the Kidstones Pass, and is the easiest motorable escape out of the valley north of Grassington. Cray's one amenity is the White Lion, an uncomplicated and welcoming hostelry with a flagged floor.

The walk from Crook Gill to Scar House is along short-cropped turf above a steep drop through ancient woodlands, the scarp being marked by limestone scars and sections of pavement. The slopes to the north rise more steadily to the height of 2109 feet on the largely unfrequented Yockenthwaite Moor.

Sentinel of the upper valley, the solidly built edifice of the Wharfedale Cairn is a notable landmark in the locality, being prominent in many views.

Beware of cars on this narrow, enclosed lane.

From Cray to Scar Top we have superlative views down the length of the dale.

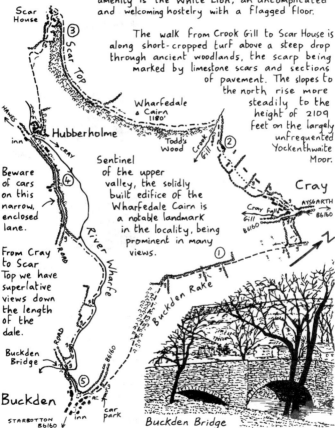

Buckden Bridge

WALK 4

| GRASS WOOD AND GHAISTRILL'S STRID |

5½ miles

from Grassington

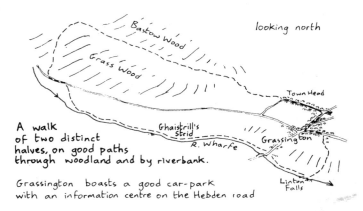

looking north

Bastow Wood

Grass Wood

Town Head

Ghaistrill's Strid

Grassington

R. Wharfe

Linton Falls

A walk
of two distinct
halves, on good paths
through woodland and by riverbank.

Grassington boasts a good car-park
with an information centre on the Hebden road

THE WALK

Leave the car park by the road into the centre of Grassington, then head up the main street past the cobbled square and the Devonshire Arms as far as a crossroads next to the institute. Here turn left along Chapel Street, and when it eventually turns sharp left, leave it by turning right into a farmyard. Bear round to the right of the main buildings to find a gate beyond the last one. A track across the field is soon vacated in order to reach a narrow gap-stile in the wall opposite, and a larger field is likewise crossed to a stile onto an enclosed track. Accompany it to its demise then take the right-hand of two facing gates to follow a wall in the same direction. At the field-end cross to a ladder-stile which admits to Grass Wood.

A good path heads up through the trees, rising steadily for about half a mile. After levelling out, two narrower paths branch right in quick succession, followed by a slight descent to a flat clearing where several tracks meet. Although this widest track we are currently on will drop down to meet the definitive path, our route proper involves retracing the few yards back to the second of those aforementioned narrower branches passed on the way to the clearing. It maintains a level course through the trees with a moss-covered limestone pavement on the left, before dropping down towards the far end of the wood. After a sharp left turn it descends more gently, merging into the wide track forsaken earlier before emerging at a stile onto Grass Wood Lane.

Head left along this quiet back road for a short distance and then take a stile into the trees on the right. The main path sets a course for the Wharfe's bank, which is accompanied downstream firstly through trees and then green pastures to the cluster of trees marking the position of the Ghaistrill's Strid. From here a string of stiles in quick succession precede more green pastures to arrive at Grassington Bridge.

Cross the road here to pass below a row of houses before regaining the same bank of the river to very soon reach the Tin Bridge at Linton Falls. After surveying the scene conclude the walk by turning up the narrow snicket from our bank, which returns us very quickly to the main car park.

Grassington Bridge

Grassington is the undisputed 'capital' of the upper Wharfedale area, a thriving community with a good range of facilities. The fine, cobbled square is the focal point but is really only the shop window: hidden away is enough interest for a day's leisurely exploration. Historically, Grassington boasted an 18th century theatre and a lead mining industry of which its nearby moor still displays much evidence. The many buildings of character include the Old Hall and the former Town Hall-cum-institute. Here also is the Upper Wharfedale Folk Museum and the headquarters of the fell rescue organisation and the National Park.

Although graced with much wooded beauty, Grass Wood is also of major importance in the botanical world, a bewildering variety of flowers being found here. It is run by the Yorkshire Naturalists' Trust. Its counterpart Bastow Wood reaches greater altitudes to the right of our path.

Where we rejoin the road stood the gibbet that hung Tom Lee, local blacksmith turned notorious murderer two centuries ago.

The large building high on the opposite bank is Netherside Hall, now a school.

In our two miles by the Wharfe we are treated to two of its rougher sections, the first being at Ghaistrill's Strid. The main feature of this loop in the river is a narrow gor though i will be general turbulence.

Beyond Grassington Bridge we pass two weirs before arriving at the less uniform delights of Linton Falls. Here the Wharfe drops loudly over a tangle of rock ledges and boulders, and is viewed dramatically from the Tin Bridge just above. New houses have replaced the former mill.

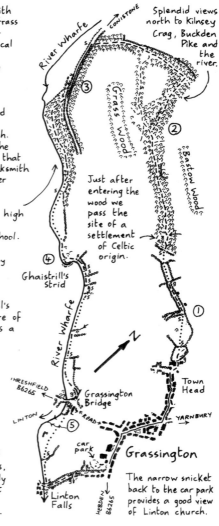

Splendid views north to Kilnsey Crag, Buckden Pike and the river.

Just after entering the wood we pass the site of a settlement of Celtic origin.

The narrow snicket back to the car park provides a good view of Linton church.

WALK 5 | BETWEEN SKIRFARE AND WHARFE

6½ miles — from Arncliffe

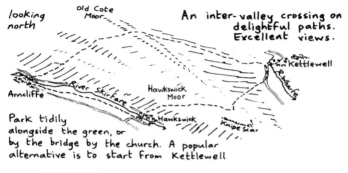

looking
north

Old Cote Moor

An inter-valley crossing on
delightful paths.
Excellent views.

Kettlewell

River Skirfare

Hawkswick Moor

Arncliffe

Hawkswick

Knipe Scar

Park tidily
alongside the green, or
by the bridge by the church. A popular
alternative is to start from Kettlewell

THE WALK

From the village green take the Litton (up-dale) road,
past the church and across the bridge over the Skirfare.
At once leave the road by a stile on the right to accompany
the river downstream, but only a short distance to another
stile onto a narrow road. From the stile opposite a good path
rises diagonally through two fields to enter a wood, continuing
up through the trees to leave by negotiating a limestone scar
at the top.

Still maintaining the same course, the path resumes
in easier vein: at a gateway in a collapsing wall a short level
section precedes the final pull, and at the second of a pair
of neighbouring stiles the ridge-wall on Old Cote Moor is gained.
The descent to Kettlewell commences immediately, the slightly
less clear path inclining to the right to eventually locate a
stile in a wall descending from the moor-top. Continuing down
at a similar angle a plateau briefly interrupts the drop before
squeezing through 'The Slit', a well-used way through a narrow
band of limestone. The path then drops down to merge with
another before reaching a gate onto the road at the entrance
to Kettlewell.

The route now lies along to the right, though this
opportunity to break the journey may well be snatched first. On
leaving the village return over the bridge and follow the road
a short distance as far as a gate and footpath sign pointing
up to the right. A good path heads away, bearing right at a

fork and then rising through trees to a level enclosure. Bearing up to the right beneath a pinewood a stile will be found in the top corner of the field, with another one just above it. The path then rises through a low scar and continues climbing steadily to a cairn marking the highest point of this crossing.

From the cairn the path undulates across to a stile in the ridge-wall. Just beyond is another cairn from where the path turns sharply right to begin its descent into Littondale. A nice easy drop down concludes by entering Hawkswick enclosed by walls. Turn right past the houses to arrive at a footbridge, and on crossing it take a stile on the right to accompany the Skirfare upstream.

This level return to Arncliffe is fairly straightforward, with an assortment of stiles and gates to point the way. For the most part the river keeps its distance, but it returns for the last third of a mile to usher us back into the village, a gate by a barn preceding a short drive to emerge by the church.

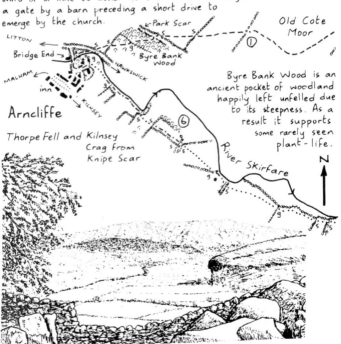

Park Scar

Old Cote Moor

LITTON

Bridge End

Byre Bank Wood

HAWKSWICK

MALHAM

inn

KILNSEY

Arncliffe

Thorpe Fell and Kilnsey Crag from Knipe Scar

Byre Bank Wood is an ancient pocket of woodland happily left unfelled due to its steepness. As a result it supports some rarely seen plant-life.

River Skirfare

N

Arncliffe is one of the most attractive yet least spoilt villages in the Dales, and is regarded as the 'capital' of Littondale. A variety of characterful greystone houses stand back in relaxed manner from a spacious green. The unpretentious inn maintains this mood, and is in fact the only hostelry in the area to serve its ale in that unrivalled fashion, directly from the barrel.

Out of sight of the green is the church of St. Oswald, which has found its own niche, embowered in trees in a truly beautiful riverside setting. Though largely rebuilt last century, the solid tower dates back 500 years. Inside is a list of the Littondale men who marched off to fight at Flodden Field in 1513.

Across the shapely bridge, the house at Bridge End played host to Charles Kingsley during his 'Water Babies' period.

Kettlewell (see Walk 10)

Old Cote Moor

The Slit

②

③

On the climb from Kettlewell note the chapel at Scargill House, somehow managing to blend into the scene.

Less than two miles below Hawkswick the Skirfare merges with the Wharfe, and during this walk we are treated to unparalleled vistas of substantial lengths of these twin-like dales immediately above their confluence. In both cases flat valley floors give way to equally well-defined slopes.

Above Arncliffe a major feature is the deep-cut Cowside Beck just behind the village, while on gaining the moor-top Buckden Pike dominates the scene with uniform-looking villages at its foot. Great Whernside rises above Kettlewell, while the lower ridge crossing permits more intimate views down Wharfedale.

ARNCLIFFE

⑤

Hawkswick

Hawkswick Moor

1240'

River Skirfare

KILNSEY

Knipe Scar

N

Hawkswick is the Skirfare's last village, and being the only one off the 'main' up-dale road it remains wonderfully undisturbed.

WALK 6

CAPPLESTONE GATE AND CONISTONE DIB

7½ miles

From Conistone

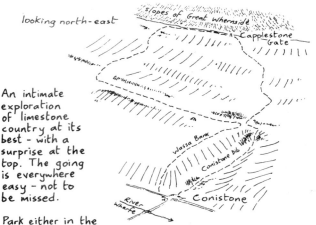

looking north-east

An intimate
exploration
of limestone
country at its
best - with a
surprise at the
top. The going
is everywhere
easy - not to
be missed.

Park either in the
village centre (fairly
limited) or on the wide section of road towards the bridge.
Alternative start: the B6160 at Kilnsey, across the valley.

THE WALK

From the road junction outside the post office set
off along the Kettlewell road, and immediately turn right on a
track across a wide 'green'. From the gate at the far end bear
right between two old caravans, a clear path materialising and
becoming stony underfoot as it heads up the dry valley of the
Dib. After being tightly confined by the imposing buttresses of
Gurling Trough the path emerges into the open to pass through
a long, green pasture. When the slopes close in again stay with
the wall for a short, stony climb to the head of the valley.

At the very top the wall is crossed by a stile as it
abuts onto a cliff: just above take a stile on the right, and
then turn left on a track to a gate which gives access to the
wide track known as Bycliffe Road. Turn right along here, and
shortly after becoming enclosed leave it by a gate on the left
just as it bends sharp right. A tractor-track crosses the field
towards a small plantation, passing to the right of it before
rising to the far end of a prominent scar. From a gateway the

path rises a little more gently to approach the white Ordnance Survey column at Capplestone Gate.

After a well-earned rest resume the walk by taking the stile by the gate and turning left along a sketchy path which remains close to the wall running along the bottom edge of the moor. An area rich in relics of the mining industry is encountered, followed by some modest gritstone outcrops. When the wall rejoins us a solid cairn is passed, and a little further a stile in the wall is used to leave the moor. After an initially steep descent the path drops leisurely through a collapsed wall and on through a long pasture. At a sketchy fork bear left, remaining in the same pasture bear right near the bottom to leave by a gate near the corner. A track then descends half-right towards a gate into a plantation.

Do not enter the trees however, but instead turn sharp left on a path which bears to the right of an increasing scar to commence a long, level section. A stile in a cross-wall is the first of five, and although the path is not always clear underfoot, the route is in no doubt. The final stile is adjacent to Conistone Pie, beyond which another scar materialises to usher us back to rejoin the Bycliffe Road above Conistone Dib.

Now turn right along it, soon descending Wassa Bank past the T.V. mast which has been in sight at various stages of the walk. Soon becoming surfaced, the access road leads down to join the Conistone-Kettlewell road, with the village only minutes along to the left.

In Conistone Dib

Conistone is an attractive little village fortunately avoided by the main road which heads updale just half a mile distant, across the river at Kilnsey: even from this distance the famous crag loses none of its grandeur. Every piece of stone in Conistone's cottages matches the natural landscape of the village's hinterland. Though restored a century ago, the hidden church retains some Norman features.

St. Mary's, Conistone

After the wonders of dazzling limestone it comes as quite a surprise to meet the sombre gritstone of Capplestone Gate. If our goal had been a hundred feet lower we would not have left limestone, but this dramatic transformation at the 1600 foot contour gives us a stroll among boulders and old mine workings in complete contrast to the rest of the journey.

As might be expected Capplestone Gate is a highly extensive viewpoint, and could well qualify as the best all-round vantage point for the varied Wharfedale scene. The fell country to the west includes, clockwise; Simon's Seat, Thorpe Fell Top, Cracoe Fell, Pendle Hill, Parson's Pulpit, Fountains Fell, Penyghent, Plover Hill, Birks Fell, Yockenthwaite Moor, Buckden Pike and Great Whernside. of which our viewpoint is a shoulder.

N

KETTLEWELL

⑦

Wassa Bank

River Wharfe

KILNSEY

Gurling Trough

GRASSINGTON

Conistone

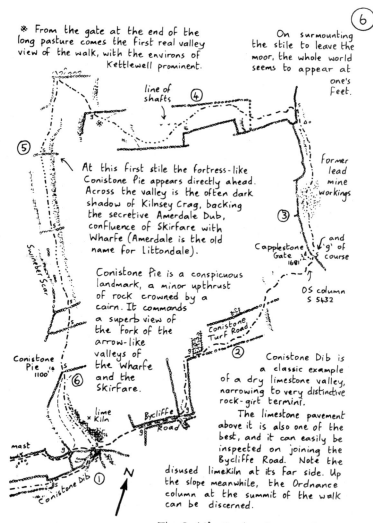

✳ From the gate at the end of the long pasture comes the first real valley view of the walk, with the environs of Kettlewell prominent.

On surmounting the stile to leave the moor, the whole world seems to appear at one's feet.

line of shafts ④

⑤

At this first stile the fortress-like Conistone Pie appears directly ahead. Across the valley is the often dark shadow of Kilnsey Crag, backing the secretive Amerdale Dub, confluence of Skirfare with Wharfe (Amerdale is the old name for Littondale).

former lead mine workings

③

Capplestone Gate 1681'

and 'g' of course

OS column S 5432

Conistone Pie is a conspicuous landmark, a minor upthrust of rock crowned by a cairn. It commands a superb view of the fork of the arrow-like valleys of the Wharfe and the Skirfare.

Swineber Scar

Conistone Turf Road

②

Conistone Pie 1100'

⑥

lime × Kiln

Bycliffe Road

Conistone Dib is a classic example of a dry limestone valley, narrowing to very distinctive rock-girt termini.

The limestone pavement above it is also one of the best, and it can easily be inspected on joining the Bycliffe Road. Note the disused limekiln at its far side. Up the slope meanwhile, the Ordnance column at the summit of the walk can be discerned.

mast

Conistone Dib ①

N

The Bycliffe Road continues to lonely Mossdale, then crosses bleak moors to Middlesmoor in Nidderdale.

31

WALK 7   **LANGERTON HILL AND DIBBLE'S BRIDGE**

6 miles   from Burnsall

A circuit of Barben Beck over gently rolling hills, with a fine stretch of the Wharfe to finish

Burnsall has a sizeable car park at the entrance to the village, added to which a riverside meadow is often opened up to supplement it. (fee at both)

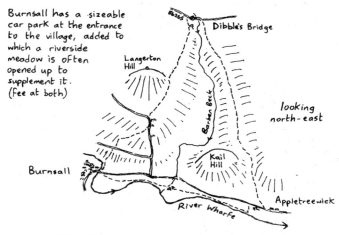

looking north-east

THE WALK

Leave Burnsall by crossing the bridge and using the steps on the left to descend to the river. After two stiles near the river climb directly up the very steep field to a stile onto the narrow Skuff Road. From the stile opposite climb another field to a stile and on to another in the very corner ahead. Now rise diagonally across a large field to a stile onto another road. Turn up it only as far as a sharp bend, and then leave by a stile directly ahead. After a continual rise up the sides of two fields, the brow of Langerton Hill is gained just below its highest point.

Our route, meanwhile, resumes its original direction from the last stile and continues to follow the right-hand wall away to a stile in it. Remain near the wall to descend a large field to a tiny stream at the far end. From the stile behind it rise half-right to a stile near a barn, then accompany the right-hand wall up to another barn. From two neighbouring stiles continue with the wall now on the left to arrive at Turf Gate

Farm. Head straight on past all the buildings to follow its access road out onto the Grassington-Pateley Bridge road.

Turn right along the road which very soon drops down to cross Dibble's Bridge, immediately after which a stile gives access to a beckside area of limestone outcrops. Vacate it by a stile in the far top corner, and continue along to a gate directly ahead. Continue straight across to a stile ahead to enter a large expanse of untamed pasture sloping down to Barben Beck. A tiny beck across our path is followed by a long, level section on a reasonably clear route high above the beck.

When a wall appears in front the path fades, but simply deflect left of it to suddenly be confined by stone walls. Escape along a short, narrow passage on the left, and on emerging turn right with the wall to eventually join an enclosed track across our way. Cross straight over to enter another long, narrow pasture, and by the opposite corner a wide track has materialised. It now gets enclosed by walls to soon drop down onto the road at one end of Appletreewick village, rather conveniently adjacent to one of its two hostelries.

From here turn right (away from the village) past Low Hall to locate an enclosed path leading down to the river. Turn right to follow the Wharfe upstream. When the river takes a big swing to the left, we are deflected right by an intervening wall to enter the farmyard at Woodhouse. When its access track turns right to join the road, go straight ahead to a footbridge and on again to a stile. The river is rejoined and soon leads back to Burnsall, omitting a final loop to cross the last field to a stile at the start of the bridge.

Ordnance Survey column,
Langerton Hill

For its modest altitude Langerton Hill is an extensive viewpoint. At the top end of Wharfedale are the summits of Buckden Pike and Great Whernside, with Simon's Seat and Burnsall Fell dominating the immediate vicinity. To the west are the heights beyond Malham and those of Malham Moor. Note also the dam of Grimwith Reservoir.

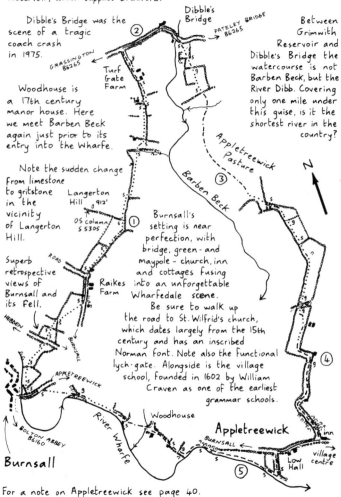

A mile north of Dibble's Bridge is the recently enlarged Grimwith Reservoir, which supplies Bradford.

Dibble's Bridge was the scene of a tragic coach crash in 1975.

Woodhouse is a 17th century manor house. Here we meet Barben Beck again just prior to its entry into the Wharfe.

Note the sudden change from limestone to gritstone in the vicinity of Langerton Hill.

Superb retrospective views of Burnsall and its Fell.

Between Grimwith Reservoir and Dibble's Bridge the watercourse is not Barben Beck, but the River Dibb. Covering only one mile under this guise, is it the shortest river in the country?

Burnsall's setting is near perfection, with bridge, green - and maypole - church, inn and cottages fusing into an unforgettable Wharfedale scene.

Be sure to walk up the road to St. Wilfrid's church, which dates largely from the 15th century and has an inscribed Norman font. Note also the functional lych-gate. Alongside is the village school, founded in 1602 by William Craven as one of the earliest grammar schools.

Dibble's Bridge

PATELEY BRIDGE B6265

GRASSINGTON B6265

Turf Gate Farm

Appletreewick Pasture

Barben Beck

N

Langerton Hill 912'

OS column S 5305

ROAD

HEBDEN

BURNSALL

Raikes Farm

APPLETREEWICK

BOLTON ABBEY B6160

River Wharfe

Woodhouse

BURNSALL

Appletreewick

inn

village centre

Low Hall

Burnsall

For a note on Appletreewick see page 40.

WALK 8

8 miles

AROUND PENYGHENT GILL

From Litton

A fine circuit of a
lively beck, and
a superb
green road

looking
south

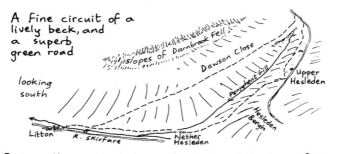

Park on the roadside either in the vicinity of the inn, or further along the road in the village 'centre'.

THE WALK

From the inn head west through the village and leave the road just beyond the 'phone box, down a drive to the left immediately before two barns usher the road out of Litton. Bear left of a short wall to a narrow wooden footbridge across the river Skirfare, then head for a gapstile just to the right. Two fields are then diagonally crossed to a pair of barns in the corner of the second. From a gate by the main barn turn right to join an enclosed track, which is then followed along to the right to arrive alongside New Bridge.

Without crossing the bridge keep straight on to a gate in front, from where a rough track climbs the hillside. This is to be our return route, but for the moment make use of only a few yards of it then break off across the field to locate a footgate in the wall ahead. After the next field a pleasant walled section returns us to the water's edge, though it is no longer the Skirfare but Hesleden Beck just short of its confluence with the river. As Nether Hesleden is approached a bridge conveys us over the beck, then turn sharp left through a gate onto the access road to the farm.

Keep left to pass between the buildings to a gate from where a track climbs to another gate. From the adjacent stile a narrow trod accompanies a fence as it rises unceasingly above the beck, eventually swinging sharp right to join the fell-road out of Halton Gill. Turn left along it as far as the first cattle-grid (a matter of a few yards), and beyond it turn down to a gate in the wall below. Drop a little further and then turn right on an increasingly clear trod, parallel with the gill throughout a splendid length.

Eventually the enclosures below Penyghent House are skirted to arrive at a mini-ravine beneath a cave entrance. On entering a larger pasture maintain the same course, closing in on the head of the gill and crossing a rocky tributary to arrive at a gate back onto the road. Turn left again for about five minutes to reach a guidepost indicating a bridle-road to Litton.

With full steam ahead this wonderful track transports us unerringly back to New Bridge, and the opening half-mile then leads equally clearly back to the village.

Penyghent from above Penyghent Gill

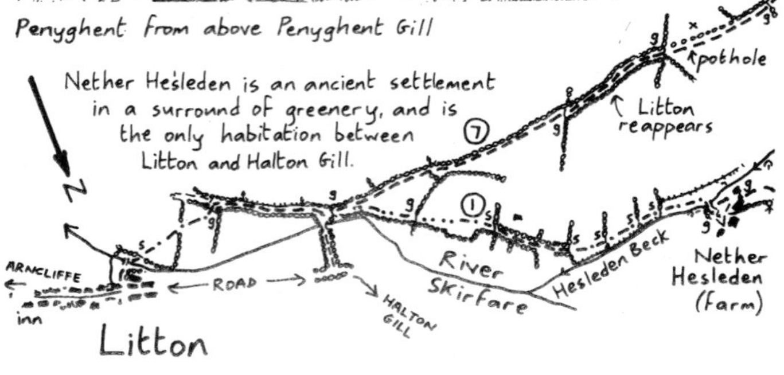

Nether Hesleden is an ancient settlement in a surround of greenery, and is the only habitation between Litton and Halton Gill.

N

pothole

Litton reappears

River Skirfare

Hesleden Beck

Nether Hesleden (farm)

ARNCLIFFE inn

ROAD

HALTON GILL

Litton

The bridle-road across Dawson Close is an outstanding example of a green road which, fortunately, like many packhorse routes escaped being surfaced, to remain as one of the most distinguishable features of the Yorkshire Dales. Evidence of its road status can be found on signposts at either end – where it meets the valley road beyond New Bridge a forlorn roadsign of not-too-distant origin points the seven miles to Stainforth.

Needless to say it provides some splendid views, firstly to Halton Gill and the head of Littondale, and later down to Litton and beyond.

Another major feature of the walk is the extended opportunity to survey Penyghent from a lesser known angle. At 2273 feet this crouching lion looks over half of the walk.

Penyghent Gill is a lovely beck, but like much of today's water it is often under the ground!

Litton is only the second largest village in the valley of the Skirfare, but can boast that it gave its name to the valley once known as Amerdale. Its attractive buildings are strung along the road from the unspoilt, whitewashed Queens Arms at the eastern end.

Rising immediately behind, and seen to good advantage on the return leg, is Birks Fell, at 2001' surely the most innocuous of all Yorkshire's mountains. An imperceptible rise marks the highest point of a ridge stretching over 11 miles from Knipe Scar in the east to an arbitrary conclusion in Ribblesdale, beyond the wilds of Cosh.

✳ At this point Penyghent appears, soon followed by Fountains Fell up to the left, above our return route.

STAINFORTH

1370'

④

Giant's Grave

ancient burial mound

Falls

Penyghent Gill

cave

Penyghent House (Farm)

⑤

limekiln

1375

N

Upper Hesleden

③

⑥

limekiln

②

Hesleden Beck

Hesleden Bergh

HALTON GILL

Dawson Close

WALK 9

7½ miles

from Appletreewick

Exceptional river scenery
precedes one of
Craven's best
limestone features

looking
north

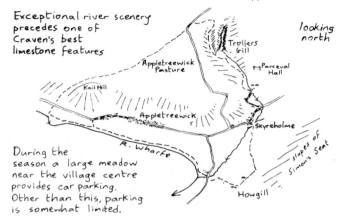

During the
season a large meadow
near the village centre
provides car parking.
Other than this, parking
is somewhat limited.

THE WALK

Leave Appletreewick by heading west out of the village on the Burnsall road, past the two inns and Low Hall to reach a walled path leading down to the Wharfe. Turn left alongside the river, though almost immediately deflected away from it, albeit breifly, through a succession of gates. On regaining the riverbank it is now clung to faithfully, through a couple of pastures before entering a delightfully wooded section. At its far end forsake the river by striking half-left across a field to join a track out onto a narrow road at a bridge.

Cross the bridge and leave the road in favour of an enclosed track up to the left. At the top a rough lane is joined alongside the farm at Howgill: turn left along it past the caravan site at Howgill Lodge. A little beyond a barn go through a gate on the left opposite an old milestone, and head away alongside the wall, first on its right, then its left. After a gateway slope down the field to a stile in the next wall, and continue down to cross a tiny beck behind which is another stile. Remain close to the main beck on the left now to soon arrive at a footbridge. Cross it and rise through a housing development to emerge onto the road at Skyreholme.

Turn right along this quiet road, forking left at a bridge to the road end at the entrance to Parceval Hall. Take the gate just before the wooden bridge to follow Skyreholme Beck upstream, a good path encountering three stiles before forking in the amphitheatre in front of Trollers Gill. The high wedge of Middle Hill divides the gorge from its parallel valley to the left: it is through this deep side-valley that the walk continues, for unfortunately the inviting entrance to Trollers Gill just across to the right is not actually on a definitive right-of-way.

Trollers Gill

Our path therefore is the nonetheless still attractive green one which rises very gently to enter the environs of a former lead-mining site. Here the way becomes a wider track (the old access road), climbing more steeply away from the mine. When it makes a sharp turn right, leave it by continuing straight ahead (left) past the deep pothole of Hell Hole. Skirting a marshy area, swing left to approach the wall in front, soon reaching a stile onto the back road from Appletreewick up to the Pateley Bridge road.

Follow this road to the left, and a little beyond a bend take a gate on the right. A wide stony track takes us across the moorland of Appletreewick Pasture, eventually dropping gently down through two stiles by gates to the bottom corner of a field. Here leave the track in favour of a gate across to the right, from where a short walled section leads down to a crossroads of paths.

At this junction (unless time is pressing) ignore

the Appletreewick sign and take the gate directly ahead to run alongside a wall to two prominent barns. Initially enclosed by walls a track runs along to the right, soon descending to join the Appletreewick-Burnsall road. Cross straight over and down the access track to Woodhouse Farm, turning to the left between the buildings to then make a bee-line for the riverbank.

All that now remains is to accompany the Wharfe downstream, to return fairly shortly to the enclosed path by which we gained the river at the start of the walk. Retrace those early steps to therefore conclude the jaunt.

Appletreewick has several claims to fame, even though many visitors may best remember its delightful name. Here are three halls and two inns in amongst a wonderful assortment of cottages. All stand on or about the narrow road wandering through the village, from High Hall at the top - note the tiny church nearby - to Low Hall at the very bottom. Probably the oldest however is the curiously named Mock Beggar Hall, a fine little edifice that once went by the title of Monk's Hall.

Of the two hostelries, one takes its name from the family of William Craven, a Dick Whittington character who found his fortune in London, becoming Lord Mayor in 1611. Not forgetting his beginnings he became a worthy local benefactor, having Burnsall's grammar school and a number of bridges in the district built. The New Inn, meanwhile, achieved national fame in recent years thanks to the enterprising 'no-smoking' policy of a previous landlord. Today it is equally enterprising in its extensive range of fascinating beers from abroad.

Trollers Gill is a magnificent limestone gorge, often known as the 'Gordale of Wharfedale'. Though not particularly tall, the cliffs remain virtually unbroken for some distance, and the narrow passage between is usually dry and safe. It is renowned as the home of the legendary 'Barguest', a spectral hound with eyes like saucers.

Descending Kail Lane note the big house in the trees across the beck: this is Hartlington Hall.

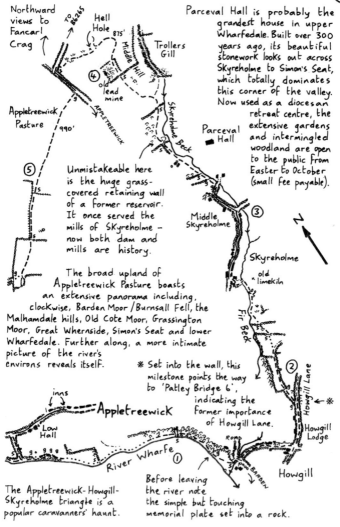

Northward views to Fancarl Crag

TO B6265

Hell Hole

875'

Middle Hill

Trollers Gill

old lead mine

④

APPLETREEWICK

Appletreewick Pasture

990'

Skyreholme Beck

Parceval Hall

Parceval Hall is probably the grandest house in upper Wharfedale. Built over 300 years ago, its beautiful stonework looks out across Skyreholme to Simon's Seat, which totally dominates this corner of the valley. Now used as a diocesan retreat centre, the extensive gardens and intermingled woodland are open to the public from Easter to October (small fee payable).

N

⑤

Unmistakeable here is the huge grass-covered retaining wall of a former reservoir. It once served the mills of Skyreholme – now both dam and mills are history.

Middle Skyreholme

③

Skyreholme

old limekiln

The broad upland of Appletreewick Pasture boasts an extensive panorama including, clockwise, Barden Moor / Burnsall Fell, the Malhamdale hills, Old Cote Moor, Grassington Moor, Great Whernside, Simon's Seat and lower Wharfedale. Further along, a more intimate picture of the river's environs reveals itself.

Fir Beck

※ Set into the wall, this milestone points the way to 'Patley Bridge 6', indicating the former importance of Howgill Lane.

②

Howgill Lane

※

inns

Appletreewick

Low Hall

Howgill Lodge

Road

River Wharfe

①

BARDEN

Howgill

The Appletreewick-Howgill-Skyreholme triangle is a popular caravanners' haunt.

Before leaving the river note the simple but touching memorial plate set into a rock.

WALK 10

5 miles

ABOVE THE WHARFE TO STARBOTTON

from Kettlewell

After an early climb
this is an easy walk
circling the
river and
giving fine
views both
up and down
the valley

Use the
village
centre
car park

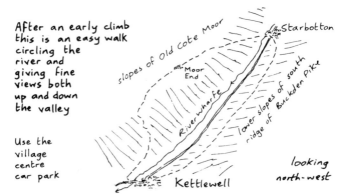

THE WALK

Leave Kettlewell by crossing the main bridge at the southern entrance to the village, then almost immediately forsake the road for the second (higher) of two gates on the right. From it a good level path heads away, ignoring the Arncliffe branch which starts climbing to the left almost at once. The path on which we remain is the access track for Moor End: after a level section it bears left in front of a clump of trees, crosses a tiny beck and then commences a well graded climb up the hillside. In no time at all it resumes its level course to run pleasantly along to Moor End.

Enter the farmyard and turn left to accompany the wall rising away from the main building. From the gate at the end continue on the level alongside a right-hand wall, using a gap part-way along before resuming the same course. From another gap at the far end keep on to a stile, and stay with the right-hand wall to a stile and gate in it. Within yards the path begins its straightforward sloping descent to the valley bottom, passing through a wood on the way. By a barn at the bottom it swings right to a footbridge over the Wharfe, a track then leading onto the road on the edge of Starbotton.

Walk a yard or two to the right and then up the lane opposite, using a gate on the right to commence a return to Kettlewell. Follow a track up through three small pastures

42

to enter one with a barn in it, then take a gate just to its left. Now turn right alongside the wall to begin a long, easy march through innumerable pastures, punctuated by a succession of stiles in intervening walls. Throughout its course the path remains virtually level and clear, with a line of unsightly telegraph poles playing their part in pointing the way.

When Kettlewell finally appears just ahead the path descends a little towards it, and the village is entered by a turn down to the right to a stile onto a short-lived enclosed path. This debouches onto a back road in the village : turn right for the quickest way back onto the main road through Kettlewell.

Fox and Hounds,
Starbotton

Kettlewell is the hub of the upper dale, a junction of roads and natural halting place. It stands on what was a major coaching route to Richmond, and the two inns at the entrance to the village would have serviced the weary travellers. The route in question is now a surfaced road, but still provides a tortuous way over Park Rash and into Coverdale. Shops, tearooms a third inn and plentiful accommodation - including a youth hostel - add more life to a village being steadily engulfed by holiday homes.

Kettlewell straddles its own beck which largely drains the slopes of Great Whernside, very much Kettlewell's mountain. These slopes bear the scars of lead mining, the one-time main industry now replaced by tourism as a partner to farming. Some delectable cottages and gardens line the beck as it races through the village.

Footpaths positively radiate from Kettlewell to all points of the compass, and one could spend a richly-varied holiday week here without the need of any transport. Just set off in a new direction!

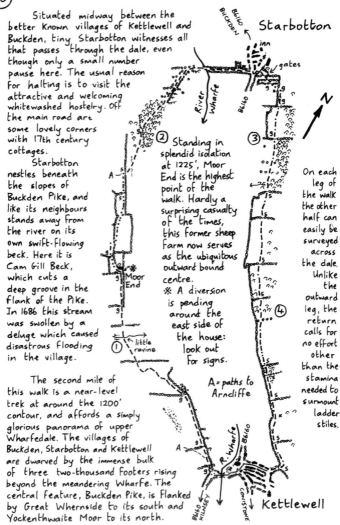

Situated midway between the better known villages of Kettlewell and Buckden, tiny Starbotton witnesses all that passes through the dale, even though only a small number pause here. The usual reason for halting is to visit the attractive and welcoming whitewashed hostelry. Off the main road are some lovely corners with 17th century cottages.

Starbotton nestles beneath the slopes of Buckden Pike, and like its neighbours stands away from the river on its own swift-flowing beck. Here it is Cam Gill Beck, which cuts a deep groove in the flank of the Pike. In 1686 this stream was swollen by a deluge which caused disastrous flooding in the village.

The second mile of this walk is a near-level trek at around the 1200' contour, and affords a simply glorious panorama of upper Wharfedale. The villages of Buckden, Starbotton and Kettlewell are dwarfed by the immense bulk of three two-thousand footers rising beyond the meandering Wharfe. The central feature, Buckden Pike, is flanked by Great Whernside to its south and Yockenthwaite Moor to its north.

② Standing in splendid isolation at 1225', Moor End is the highest point of the walk. Hardly a surprising casualty of the times, this former sheep farm now serves as the ubiquitous outward bound centre.
※ A diversion is pending around the east side of the house: look out for signs.

A = paths to Arncliffe

On each leg of the walk the other half can easily be surveyed across the dale. Unlike the outward leg, the return calls for no effort other than the stamina needed to surmount ladder stiles.

Starbotton

Moor End

① little ravine

Kettlewell

WALK 11

THE WHARFE AT BOLTON ABBEY

4½ miles

from Bolton Abbey!

A simple riverside stroll on good paths in splendid surroundings. The central feature, in sight for much of the walk, is the hoary old ruin of Upper Wharfedale's most famous building.

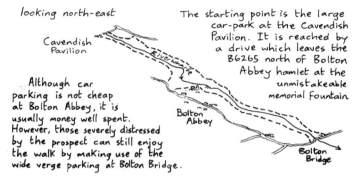

looking north-east

Cavendish Pavilion

River Wharfe

Bolton Abbey

Bolton Bridge

The starting point is the large car-park at the Cavendish Pavilion. It is reached by a drive which leaves the B6265 north of Bolton Abbey hamlet at the unmistakeable memorial fountain.

Although car parking is not cheap at Bolton Abbey, it is usually money well spent. However, those severely distressed by the prospect can still enjoy the walk by making use of the wide verge parking at Bolton Bridge.

THE WALK

From the Cavendish Pavilion set off back along the drive, but from the gate by the cattle-grid go left into the car park and follow the extended car park access track along the bank of the Wharfe. When the track ends keep company with the river until the pasture abruptly ends, then climb to a stile to emerge onto the road at the Cavendish Memorial.

Turn left for only a couple of minutes to a gate into the priory grounds: the most direct route back towards the river is down through the graveyard, but surely few will not halt to explore the ruins and the priory church. On arriving at the wooden footbridge and its adjacent stepping stones do not be tempted to cross, but instead follow the river downstream again. A long, pleasant pasture now leads all the way to Bolton Bridge, the river being crossed in safety by a footbridge in its shadow.

Within yards turn left along an enclosed way between a cottage and Red Lion Farm, to enter a riverside pasture. As the Wharfe is neared we are deflected around a steep, wooded bank, then drop back down to cross three pastures, parallel with the nearby Wharfe. After a tiny beck and a step-stile a field is climbed, remaining with the left-hand fence to a stile and a superb high-level vantage point.

From the stile a good path runs along to the right, being joined by another as it heads through the trees a fair way above the river. The path ends on meeting a narrow road as it prepares to ford Pickles Beck: a footbridge caters for dry-shod pedestrians. On the other side a stile gives access to the riverbank for the final few minutes back to the Pavilion bridge.

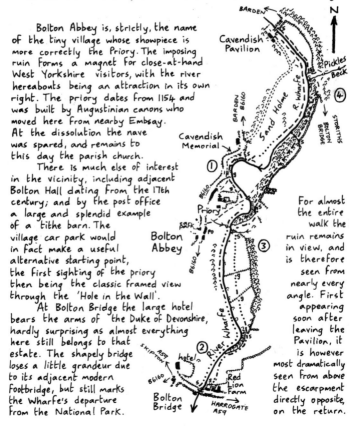

Bolton Abbey is, strictly, the name of the tiny village whose showpiece is more correctly the Priory. The imposing ruin forms a magnet for close-at-hand West Yorkshire visitors, with the river hereabouts being an attraction in its own right. The priory dates from 1154 and was built by Augustinian canons who moved here from nearby Embsay. At the dissolution the nave was spared, and remains to this day the parish church.

There is much else of interest in the vicinity, including adjacent Bolton Hall dating from the 17th century; and by the post office a large and splendid example of a tithe barn. The village car park would in fact make a useful alternative starting point, the first sighting of the priory then being the classic framed view through the 'Hole in the Wall'.

At Bolton Bridge the large hotel bears the arms of the Duke of Devonshire, hardly surprising as almost everything here still belongs to that estate. The shapely bridge loses a little grandeur due to its adjacent modern footbridge, but still marks the Wharfe's departure from the National Park.

For almost the entire walk the ruin remains in view, and is therefore seen from nearly every angle. First appearing soon after leaving the Pavilion, it is however most dramatically seen from above the escarpment directly opposite, on the return.

46

Bolton Bridge

Tithe Barn, Bolton Abbey

WALK 12

THE HEAD OF LITTONDALE

from Halton Gill

Easy walking, with good beck
scenery in typically bleak
Pennine surroundings

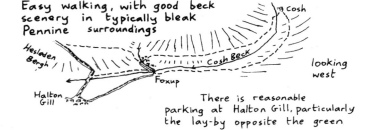

looking
west

There is reasonable
parking at Halton Gill, particularly
the lay-by opposite the green

THE WALK

From the road junction by the green turn down the
Stainforth road as far as the bridge, and immediately after it
leave by a stile on the right to descend to the river bank. Now
simply accompany the Skirfare upstream, taking in several gates
and stiles before a new path squeezes between pens and river to
emerge onto the road at Foxup Bridge. Turn right over the said
structure and then immediately left on a wide track. This rough
farm road heads unerringly up the valley, gradually rising above
Cosh Beck to eventually arrive at Cosh, the first building since
Foxup.

Without entering the confines of Cosh, turn off the
track to commence the return journey by descending towards
the beck, but only as far as the brink of the steeper drop
to the water's edge. Maintaining this level, head downstream as
far as a sizeable sheepfold which was probably seen from the
outward journey. At this point descend to the beck, fording it
and continuing downstream to an immediately intervening wall.
From the stile in it rise very slightly across the large pasture
to locate a stile in the next wall.

From here on a string of several further stiles lead
through pathless fields, virtually parallel with the beck below.
Eventually Foxup appears ahead, and from a gateway descend a
field to the nearest buildings. A stile and gate between them
give access to a track which drops down to Foxup Beck, crossing
it to the road terminus and Foxup Bridge Farm.

Do not continue to Foxup Bridge again, but take
a gate opposite the Farm and a track up the field. After a

Cosh 1400'

(2)

THE WALK (continued)

Cosh Beck

second gate the track bears across to a gate in the right-hand wall: do not use it but continue up the field, soon levelling out to arrive at a gate in the far-left corner. Remaining level a large pasture is crossed to another gate, the path then running on through low outcrops of limestone to merge with the Stainforth road.

Turn left for a straightforward descent back into Halton Gill, a clear target in the valley bottom.

(3)

(1)

←Charming scene of tiny arched bridge, lively beck and limestone ledges.

Cosh is Remote: geographically it stands at the very heart of the National Park, but it couldn't be further from the centre of things! A thriving farmstead earlier this century, it spent many unoccupied years, though it has now undergone restoration. Interestingly, Littondale's highest building is only a five mile walk from Horton-in-Ribblesdale's railway station, a trek that was undertaken by its former occupants.

The name Cosh is of Norse origin, and was also at one time a grange of Fountains Abbey.

Foxup Beck

Foxup

N

↑

Foxup Bridge

ROAD

Halton Gill

Falls→

R. Skirfare

(4)

Foxup is a farming hamlet marking the upper limit of the valley's surfaced road. At Foxup Bridge the two hitherto moorland becks combine to create the Skirfare.

Halton Gill is the first sizeable settlement in Littondale. Its cluster of grey buildings include a former chapel and a former school, late 16th/early 17th century and now serving as private dwellings.

LITTON

Halton Gill Bridge

(5)

1300'

STAINFORTH

The last couple of miles provide grand views both down the dale and also across to Halton Gill nestling beneath Horse Head Moor.

49

WALK 13

THE ENVIRONS OF HEBDEN GILL

3½ miles

from Hebden

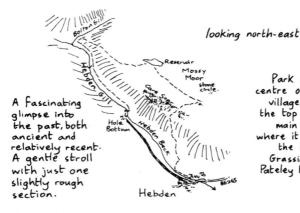

looking north-east

A fascinating glimpse into the past, both ancient and relatively recent. A gentle stroll with just one slightly rough section.

Park in the centre of the village, near the top of the main street where it joins the B6265 Grassington–Pateley Bridge road.

THE WALK

The walk begins from the top end of the village, where the main road crosses Hebden Beck just down from the inn. Take the surfaced road up the west (left) side of the beck, and remain on it for about three-quarters of a mile until arrival at the hamlet of Hole Bottom signals its demise.

The lane is replaced by a good track which forks right through a gate to drop down to cross a small bridge over Hebden Beck. This former miners' track now accompanies the beck upstream, rising gently alongside as evidence of the former lead mining industry appears. After a third gate we enter an area of spoil heaps and ruinous buildings: after the fourth and final gate the devastation is all but left behind.

A little beyond the site of a tiny reservoir on the right, the main track drops down to ford the beck before the inflowing Bolton Gill joins it. This is the turning point of the walk, so without crossing either beck, turn up an inviting path beckoning us up the slope to the right. Looking up the deep cleft of this side-valley, a dark shadow will be seen near to the top: it is a former winding shaft that has undergone a restoration.

Our return route, however, forsakes the inviting path at the first opportunity, in favour of an equally pleasant green path which curves back up to the right through the bracken. It is narrow but easy to follow, passing an old mine level before reaching a gate. This admits to an area of rough pasture, and a sketchy path maintains a near level trod through this and two further pastures, finding the exit from the third by being deflected left of a ruinous section of wall.

From the gate the path continues by the right-hand wall to the next gate ahead, but a short detour can be made to the conspicuous level outline to the left: it is the retaining wall of Mossy Moor Reservoir, another relic from the mining days. When traversed to the right, its little embankment points back to the gate ahead. Open moorland is now reached, and a good track skirts the sea of heather as we continue by the wall.

At the point where the wall turns sharp right to accommodate the access road to Scar Top House, a short section of collapsed wall strikes away towards a small stone circle, just out of sight from where we are standing. After having perhaps puzzled a little why our ancestors should ever have felt the urge to construct such a permanent feature out there, turn with the wall to follow the track in towards Scar Top House. Note that a wall-stile beyond the cattle-grid marks the actual right-of-way.

Do not enter the private yard of the house but follow its enclosing wall around to the right to arrive at a gateway, immediately beneath which is a sudden drop back into Hebden Gill. A short, steep section therefore ensues: from the gap descend by a wall on the left, on a clear path which skirts the greater part of the tangle of boulders of Care Scar just to the right — it is advisable to stand still when viewing this prospect. The descent is soon complete and the path continues through another gateway to more relaxed surroundings.

The path now becomes unclear in this grassy pasture — bear a little to the left to drop down to join the left-hand wall, and on levelling out, go left with it to a gate in the corner. Once through it go with the collapsing wall for a few yards, then cross it and the field behind it to a stile in the bottom corner. Rather cleverly it conveys us into the diagonally-opposite field, from where a path soon materialises to lead in similar direction down to rejoin Hebden Beck.

From a stile there either cross the footbridge to the road on which we began, or preferably remain on this bank down to a row of cottages and thence the road bridge in Hebden.

Winding shaft, Bolton Gill

This survivor from the lead mining days dates from around 1856, and was restored by the Earby Mines Research Group.

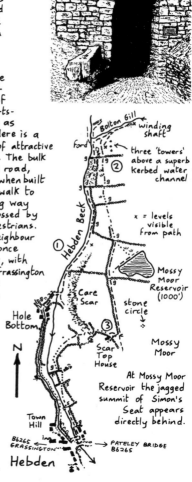

Hebden is a small village divided by the Grassington-Pateley Bridge road. North of the road - where our walk starts - is Town Hill, obviously named as the top end of the village. Here is a highly photogenic grouping of attractive cottages and an old bridge. The bulk of Hebden stands below the road, including the church which when built saved the parishioners the walk to Linton. The Wharfe is a long way below the village, and is crossed by a suspension bridge for pedestrians.

Hebden, like its bigger neighbour Grassington, grew with the once thriving lead mining industry, with Hebden Gill, and above it Grassington Moor, abounding in evocative reminders of those hard days.

Mossy Moor's stone circle is a fairly basic affair almost hidden in thick heather. It consists of four major stones, and eight in total.

Above Hole Bottom the beck is in sparkling form.

On arrival at Scar Top the dramatic view includes the bulk of Burnsall Fell and the distant outline of Pendle Hill.

Map labels:
Bolton Gill
winding shaft
ford
three 'towers' above a superb kerbed water channel
Hebden Beck
x = levels visible from path
Mossy Moor Reservoir (1000')
stone circle
Care Scar
Hole Bottom
Mossy Moor
Scar Top House
N
At Mossy Moor Reservoir the jagged summit of Simon's Seat appears directly behind.
Town Hill
B6265 GRASSINGTON
Inn
PATELEY BRIDGE B6265
Hebden

WALK 14

8½ miles

From Buckden

looking east

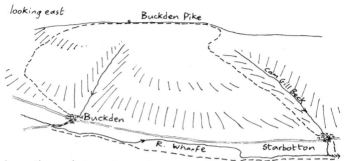

A well-graded and popular
climb to Wharfedale's second
highest summit, with the bonus
of a beautiful riverside return.

Buckden has a
large car-park.

THE WALK

     Leave the car park not by its usual exit, but instead by a gate at its northern end, from where a stony track makes its way gently up Buckden Rake. When the surround of trees disappears, the track turns right through a gate and onto the level. From the next gate however, our chosen path forks right to resume the upward push. This generally clear path rises diagonally through five pastures, and beyond the small gate after the last of them it heads more directly up the open fell. A little sketchily it crosses to a wall on the left, to then accompany it up to the cairn and Ordnance Survey column on the summit of Buckden Pike.

     To leave the top use the stile to cross the boundary wall and turn right to follow it along the broad ridge of the Pike, losing little height until passing a memorial cross. At the foot of the slope behind it the track known as the Walden Road is met at a sharp angle in the wall. Use the bridle-gate there to re-cross the wall and commence the descent to Starbotton. The way is fairly clear throughout: after sloping down across two large, rough pastures linked by a little mining debris, a cracking pace can be adopted as the track descends parallel with Cam Gill Beck to our left.

The Walden Road is a former packhorse route which continues over the fell to drop down to the head of the lonely Walden valley and ultimately Wensleydale.

BUCKDEN PIKE
2302'

boundary stone

OS column
55520

Memorial Cross

② ③

The path linking the summit and the Walden Road is not currently recorded as a definitive right-of-way.

collapsed kiln

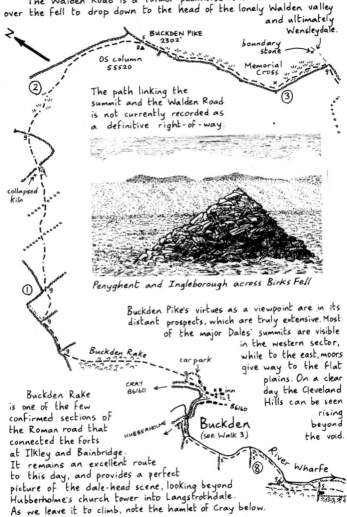

Penyghent and Ingleborough across Birks Fell

①

Buckden Pike's virtues as a viewpoint are in its distant prospects, which are truly extensive. Most of the major Dales' summits are visible in the western sector, while to the east, moors give way to the flat plains. On a clear day the Cleveland Hills can be seen rising beyond the void.

Buckden Rake

car park

CRAY
B6160

inn

B6160

Buckden Rake is one of the few confirmed sections of the Roman road that connected the forts at Ilkley and Bainbridge. It remains an excellent route to this day, and provides a perfect picture of the dale-head scene, looking beyond Hubberholme's church tower into Langstrothdale. As we leave it to climb, note the hamlet of Cray below.

HUBBERHOLME

Buckden
(see Walk 3)

⑧

River Wharfe

THE WALK continued

Starbotton is entered via a bridge onto a lane, which leads to the right and onto the main road by the Fox and Hounds. Turn left through the village, and after the last building leave the road by an enclosed track on the right, which leads to a footbridge over the Wharfe. Cross it and turn right to follow the river upstream to commence the return to Buckden.

When the Wharfe temporarily parts company the path continues straight ahead alongside a wall on the left: several stiles and gates interrupt the journey. As the river returns a wide track is joined, but as the Wharfe bends away again this time go with it to remain on its bank until Buckden Bridge is encountered. Here leave the river and cross the bridge to re-enter the village.

For a note on
Starbotton
see Walk 10

ruin

④

Cam Gill Beck

Walden Road

⑤

The long
descent to
Starbotton
is at such a
gentle gradient
that one's time
can be employed in
enjoying the splendid
views down Wharfedale.

Note the identical well-chosen
sites of the walk's two villages —
high above the river, astride fast-
flowing becks and on the sunnier side
of the valley.

The Memorial
Cross

This noble structure
was erected by a
Polish airman, lone
survivor of a
second world
war plane
crash on
the fell.

River Wharfe   Starbotton

KETTLEWELL

B6160   B6160

⑥

stepping stones

⑦   ruin   falls

55

WALK 15
9 miles

from Linton

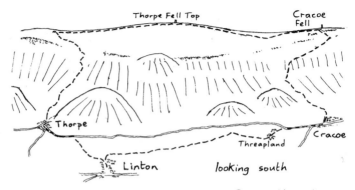

looking south

A Fine stretch of moorland rambling, contrasting well with the tiny villages under the steep slopes

Park in the village centre, either by the green or on the road through the village.

THE WALK

From the inn cross the green and the beck and follow the lane along to the right to its imminent demise at a farm. Turn left in front of a large barn and along a briefly enclosed track. At the end it climbs with the left-hand wall, and though it peters out remain with the wall to negotiate three intervening stiles. From the third head away in the same direction, rising through a large field and going left of a line of trees to a ruinous barn. A stile to the left of the barn admits onto a roughly surfaced lane. Turn left to follow its narrow course into the hamlet of Thorpe.

Bear right at the triangular junction in the centre and keep on until the road dissolves into a couple of rough tracks. Opt for the left one which climbs steeply between walls to emerge onto the open moor. Two sunken tracks head directly away from the gate, and it is the right-hand one which is to be preferred. It swings up to the right to terminate at the remains of a small quarry: here turn up to the left to head in a southerly direction, a track reappearing at a cairn. On rounding the beginnings of a beck the track regains its groove, though loses it briefly again at a faint fork. Keep right to rise up a gentle slope, and as the groove disappears for good a stone shooting house appears ahead, and is soon reached.

At the shooting house our track ends and a wider track is encountered, but unfortunately it is of little use to us. Though it can be followed a short distance to the right, it must then be forsaken in order to climb the modest slope directly behind the building. Though pathless, a short half-mile will lead to the Ordnance Survey column on Thorpe Fell Top.

After admiring the view it is necessary to engage in a further bout of heather-bashing by aiming in a south-westerly direction for the conspicuous monument on Cracoe Fell. At an inscribed boundary stone just short of the depression between the fell-top and the monument, swing right in front of a row of grouse-butts to join the substantial wall along the top of the escarpment. Now turn left on a path by the wall for an easy walk up to the monument: a stile provides access to it.

At our feet, just to the north, is Cracoe, which is the next objective. On locating the nearest group of trees this side of the village, a walled lane can also be seen running from the end of the rough pasture beneath us to the village itself. Descend the virtually pathless slope—initially with care where rocks abound—to reach the rough lane which leads unerringly into Cracoe.

Turn right along the busy main road and leave it at the first opportunity along a much pleasanter back road. This too is left at the first chance in favour of a short track to Threapland Farm on the left. After crossing the beck turn right in front of the main buildings to a gate from where an initially enclosed track heads away. When faced by a fence the track forks, and our now pathless course follows the fence around to the right to a stile. From the tiny beck behind it aim directly across two fields, then bear a little to the left above a small wood to locate the next stile.

Two narrow fields are then crossed to descend the next one to a tiny beck and an access road in front of a barn. Cross them both to a stile just left of the barn, and from the next stile follow the right-hand wall across a larger field. From the gate at the end a tractor-track leads across the final field to rejoin the track by which we left Linton. Turn left to re-enter the village and end the walk.

■ Along with Barden Fell on the opposite bank of the Wharfe, Barden Moor is also part of the Duke of Devonshire's estate, and the moorland walking between the points marked thus ✳ (ie the fell lanes out of Thorpe and Cracoe) is on access land which may be closed on certain days during the grouse shooting season. It is important to read the notes at the foot of page 5.

The little settlement of Cracoe marks the barely discernable watershed between Wharfedale and neighbouring Airedale. Its long, low, whitewashed inn has a good few years history behind it, and like several others in the vicinity it bears the arms of the family on whose moor we have just been tramping.

On departing the untidy environs of Threapland, one's eyes cannot fail to be drawn by the scene of utter devastation presented by the quarry to the left.

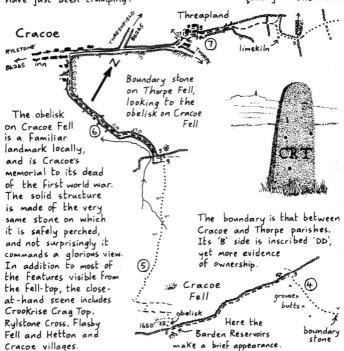

Cracoe

RYLSTONE
B6265   inn

THRESHFIELD
BRASS

Threapland

⑦

THORPE

limekiln

Boundary stone on Thorpe Fell, looking to the obelisk on Cracoe Fell

⑥

The obelisk on Cracoe Fell is a familiar landmark locally, and is Cracoe's memorial to its dead of the first world war. The solid structure is made of the very same stone on which it is safely perched, and not surprisingly it commands a glorious view. In addition to most of the features visible from the fell-top, the close-at-hand scene includes Crookrise Crag Top, Rylstone Cross, Flasby Fell and Hetton and Cracoe villages.

C R T

The boundary is that between Cracoe and Thorpe parishes. Its 'B' side is inscribed 'DD', yet more evidence of ownership.

⑤

Cracoe Fell

④

grousex butts

obelisk

1650'

boundary stone

Here the Barden Reservoirs make a brief appearance.

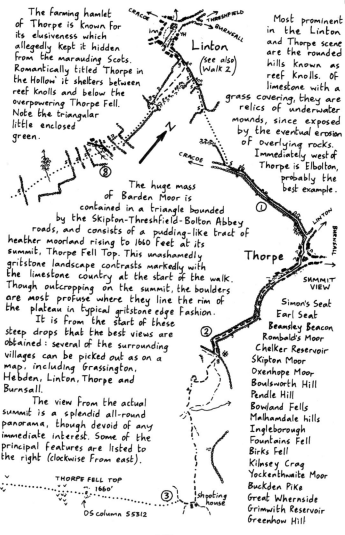

The farming hamlet of Thorpe is known for its elusiveness which allegedly kept it hidden from the marauding Scots. Romantically titled 'Thorpe in the Hollow' it shelters between reef knolls and below the overpowering Thorpe Fell. Note the triangular little enclosed green.

Most prominent in the Linton and Thorpe scene are the rounded hills known as reef knolls. Of limestone with a grass covering, they are relics of underwater mounds, since exposed by the eventual erosion of overlying rocks. Immediately west of Thorpe is Elbolton, probably the best example.

CRACOE

THRESHFIELD

BURNSALL

inn

YH

Linton

(see also) (Walk 2)

N

CRACOE

Thorpe

LINTON

BURNSALL

SUMMIT VIEW

The huge mass of Barden Moor is contained in a triangle bounded by the Skipton-Threshfield-Bolton Abbey roads, and consists of a pudding-like tract of heather moorland rising to 1660 feet at its summit, Thorpe Fell Top. This unashamedly gritstone landscape contrasts markedly with the limestone country at the start of the walk. Though outcropping on the summit, the boulders are most profuse where they line the rim of the plateau in typical gritstone edge fashion.

It is from the start of these steep drops that the best views are obtained: several of the surrounding villages can be picked out as on a map, including Grassington, Hebden, Linton, Thorpe and Burnsall.

The view from the actual summit is a splendid all-round panorama, though devoid of any immediate interest. Some of the principal features are listed to the right (clockwise from east).

Simon's Seat
Earl Seat
Beamsley Beacon
Rombald's Moor
Chelker Reservoir
Skipton Moor
Oxenhope Moor
Boulsworth Hill
Pendle Hill
Bowland Fells
Malhamdale hills
Ingleborough
Fountains Fell
Birks Fell
Kilnsey Crag
Yockenthwaite Moor
Buckden Pike
Great Whernside
Grimwith Reservoir
Greenhow Hill

THORPE FELL TOP
1660'

OS column SS312

shooting house

WALK 16

6 miles

THE ASCENT OF GREAT WHERNSIDE

from Kettlewell

A charming beckside
ramble precedes a
short and easy
fellwalk to
Wharfedale's
highest top

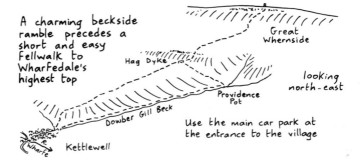

Great
Whernside

*looking
north-east*

Hag Dyke

Providence
Pot

Dowber Gill Beck

Wharfe

Kettlewell

Use the main car park at
the entrance to the village

THE WALK

From the car park head into the village and leave
the main road immediately before the bridge by the two hotels,
turning along the road to the right. Fork left at the maypole
to pass the church, and at the third inn turn sharp right
on a lane alongside the beck. At a shapely bridge and chapel
the lane becomes a track, and just a little further it crosses
Dowber Gill Beck: here leave it by turning up the little beckside
path to a gate in the adjacent wall. Now turn right to begin
a long mile and a quarter keeping very close company with
the beck. Several stiles are encountered and little height gained
until the unmistakeable site of Providence Pot is reached, crossing
the beck just before it.

Directly behind is the meeting of twin becks, but our
path is the very clear one up the left-hand slope immediately
next to the pothole. Recross the beck then, and climb the path
which soons levels out to approach Hag Dyke. Do not enter its
confines but climb the wide path up the steep scarp to a line
of cairns at the top. The summit now appears directly ahead,
and the path crosses a damp plateau before a steady climb
to the highest point.

To return to Kettlewell retrace steps to Hag Dyke and
enter its yard by a stile by the main building. Follow the access
track out to a gate, then leave it to drop half-left to eventually
meet a left-hand wall. Keep parallel with the beck far below, and
a sketchy path works its way back to the track over Dowber Gill
Beck. The finish can be varied by crossing the bridge by the chapel.

Great Whernside is not only the highest of Wharfedale's fells, it is by far the bulkiest. Only from Kettlewell is there anything like easy access. To the east innumerable square miles of bleak moorland fall to the upper reaches of Nidderdale, indeed the Nidd is born within a mile of the summit. Atop the line of Long Crags - large 'scrambling' boulders - stands an immense pile of stones, a cairn and a half. The National Park boundary runs along this summit ridge.

The view is largely one of fells, from the nearby mass of Buckden Pike to the distant Three Peaks, of which Penyghent looks particularly distinguished. A short but lovely section of Wharfedale can be seen from Kilnsey Crag to Grass Woods.

At 1525 feet, Hag Dyke is one of the highest buildings in the country. It is now put to use as a scout outdoor centre.

For a note on Kettlewell see Walk 10.

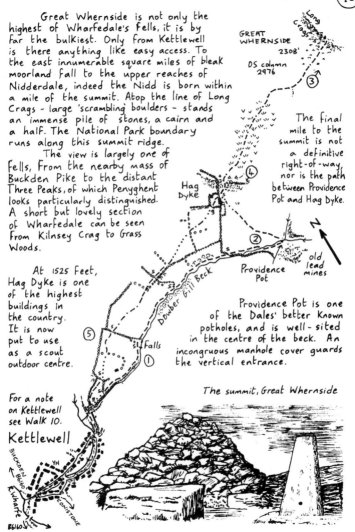

GREAT WHERNSIDE 2308'
OS column 2976
Long Crags

③

The final mile to the summit is not a definitive right-of-way, nor is the path between Providence Pot and Hag Dyke.

④

Hag Dyke

②

N

old lead mines

Providence Pot

Dowber Gill Beck

Providence Pot is one of the Dales' better known potholes, and is well-sited in the centre of the beck. An incongruous manhole cover guards the vertical entrance.

⑤

Falls ①

The summit, Great Whernside

Kettlewell

BUCKDEN BRIDGE
R.Wharfe
YH
CONISTONE
B6160

LOG OF THE WALKS

These two pages provide an opportunity to keep a permanent record of the walks completed

WALK	DATE	TIME Start	TIME Finish	WEATHER	COMMENTS
1					
2					
3					
4					
5					
6					
7					
8					

WALK	DATE	TIME Start	Finish	WEATHER	COMMENTS
9					
10					
11					
12					
13					
14					
15					
16					

KEY TO THE MAP SYMBOLS

direction of north

scale
2½ inches = 1 mile

Route   clear   sketchy
no visible path

Route on public road
wall
unenclosed   fence/hedge

River/beck   Marsh   Peat grough
bridge

Crags   Limestone clints   Loose rocks/ scree   Cairns
summit   other

Trees   Buildings   Church   Abbreviations
c = cattle grid
s = stile
g = gate

Miles from start
③

THE COUNTRY CODE

Respect the life and work of the countryside
Protect wildlife, plants and trees
Keep to public paths across farmland
Safeguard water supplies
Go carefully on country roads
Keep dogs under control
Guard against all risks of fire
Fasten all gates
Leave no litter - take it with you
Make no unnecessary noise
Leave livestock, crops and machinery alone
Use gates and stiles to cross fences, hedges
and walls